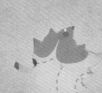

big & SMALL

Original Korean text by Ji-wu Kim
Illustrations by Annie Wilkinson
Original Korean edition © Yeowon Media Co. Ltd. 2009

This English edition published by Big & Small in 2014
by arrangement with Yeowon Media Co. Ltd.
English text edited by Joy Cowley
English edition © Big & Small 2014

ISBN: 978-1-921790-75-1
Printed in Korea

Looking for Spring

Written by Ji-wu Kim Illustrated by Annie Wilkinson
Edited by Joy Cowley

It was time for the baby bear
to have his winter sleep.

"I don't like winter sleep,"
said the baby bear.
"I am going to look for spring."

So one baby bear went off,
waddle, waddle, waddle.

Two badgers called, "Hey! Baby Bear!
Where are you going?"

"I don't like winter sleep,"
said the baby bear to the badgers.
"I'm going to look for spring."

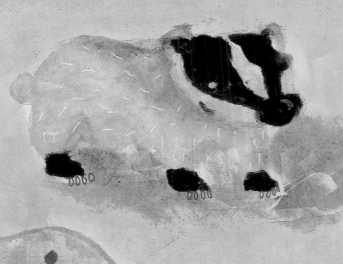

"We will help you look,"
said the two badgers.

They met three porcupines.

"We don't like winter sleep.
We are looking for spring,"
said the baby bear.

"We will help you!"
said the three porcupines.

13

Four squirrels cried,
"Us too! Us too!"

So four squirrels, three porcupines,
two badgers and one baby bear
went looking for spring.
Waddle, waddle, waddle.

Five frogs jumped out of the pond.
"We will come, too!
We will help you to look for spring."
Hop, hop, hop!

One bear,
two badgers,
three porcupines,

18

four squirrels

and five frogs

stopped.

No one knew where spring was,
and they were very sleepy.

Just then, flake by flake,
snow began to fall.

They all fell fast asleep,
and they slept for a long, long time.

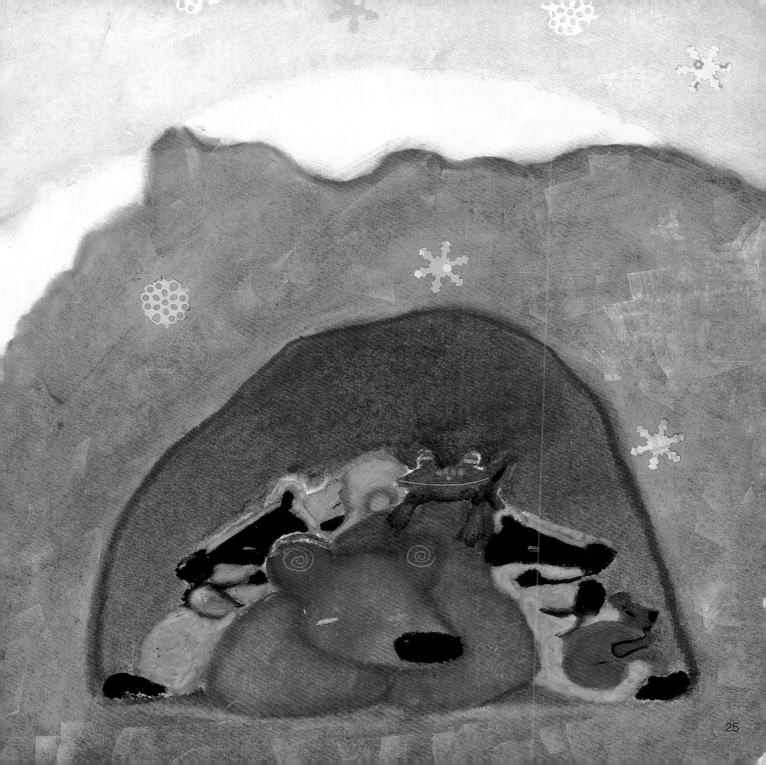

When they woke up,
they rubbed their eyes.

One bear,
two badgers,
three porcupines,
four squirrels
and five frogs
had found spring!

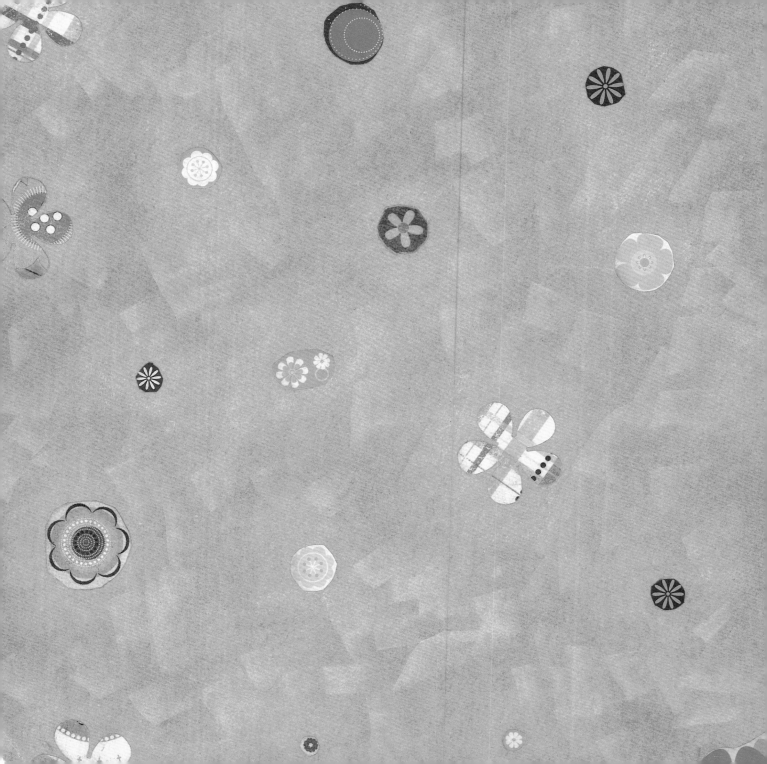

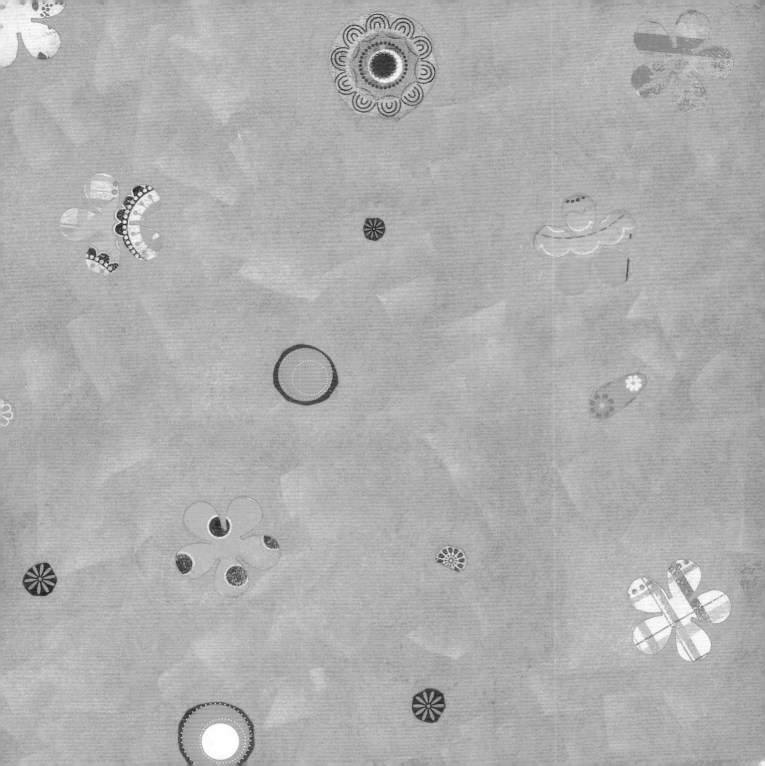